D0722022

Cosmetic Surgery for Teens

Other titles in the Teen Issues *series:*

Cosmetic Surgery for Teens

Choices and Consequences

Kathleen Winkler

Enslow Publishers, Inc.

40 Industrial Road   PO Box 38
Box 398   Aldershot
Berkeley Heights, NJ 07922   Hants GU12 6BP
USA   UK

http://www.enslow.com

Library of Congress Cataloging-in-Publication Data

Winkler, Kathleen.
    Cosmetic surgery for teens : choices and consequences / Kathleen Winkler.
        v. cm. — (Teen issues)
    Contents: Lori's story — Why do teenagers consider cosmetic surgery? —
The pros and cons of cosmetic surgery for teens — The procedures and how
they are done — Making the decision.
    ISBN 0-7660-1957-8
    1. Surgery, Plastic—Juvenile literature. 2. Teenagers—Surgery—Juvenile literature.
[1. Surgery, Plastic.] I. Title. II. Series.
    RD119.W575 2003
    617.9'5'00835—dc21

                             2002155154

Printed in the United States of America

10 9 8 7 6 5 4 3 2 1

To Our Readers:
We have done our best to make sure all Internet Addresses in this book were active and
appropriate when we went to press. However, the author and the publisher have no
control over and assume no liability for the material available on those Internet sites or
on other Web sites they may link to. Any comments or suggestions can be sent by e-mail
to comments@enslow.com or to the address on the back cover.

Illustration Credits: 2000 Corbis Corporation, pp. 11, 17, 49; Byron Medical,
Inc., p. 40; Ralph Winkler, pp. 29, 33, 44, 51.

Cover Illustration: Alex Bartel/Science Photo Library

Contents

1

Lori's Story

Lori was born with a larger-than-average nose. Nothing terrible—she did not look grotesque. But it was big enough that she felt uncomfortable with it and the other kids teased her.

"'Big nose, big nose,' that's what they called me starting in about fourth grade," she says. "Kids can be so mean to each other. I'd come home crying from school. I remember looking in the mirror and thinking, 'Gee, I really do have a big nose.'"

When Lori got to high school, the kids were not as obvious with their teasing. Yet she always felt that she was not as attractive as the other girls despite her pretty blond hair and big blue eyes.

"By the end of my junior year I was seriously thinking about having cosmetic surgery on my nose," she says. "When I started my senior year, I decided that's what I wanted for my graduation present. When my parents asked what I wanted for graduation, I told them. My sister had gotten a car; I said I wanted plastic surgery. They looked surprised but just said, 'Oh, well, OK.' They didn't make much of a fuss. That really surprised me because it took me forever to convince them to let me get my ears pierced!"

Lori and her mother visited a cosmetic surgeon for his opinion. He suggested that by filling out Lori's receding chin at the same time as her nose was made smaller, her face would be more in balance. That would make her new nose look even better.

"I wasn't ever nervous about having it done because I was still at the age when you think that nothing can ever go wrong," she says. "They told me about all the risks, but kids just kind of tune that stuff out. You just know that what you want is what's going to be. But my mom was fully aware of the risks!"

Still, her mother did not try to talk Lori out of the surgery. The doctor took photos of Lori's face from many angles and explained, using the photos, what he was going to do. Lori's surgery took place before doctors had the computers they use now to show patients what they will look like after surgery.

They scheduled the surgery at a day-surgery clinic for right after graduation. "I wanted things to be completely healed before I went to college, so I wanted to do it right away," Lori says. "I wasn't scared at all. I was more excited about it—'Hey, I'm going to go get a new nose today! Great!'"

Lori's mother was with her when they were getting her ready for surgery, she remembers. "I never felt anything. I don't even remember them taking me into the operating room," she says.

The surgery was done with incisions, the cuts doctors make with a scalpel, on the inside and outside of her nose.

There was another on the inside of her lip to place some cartilage from her nose into her chin. (Cartilage is the rubbery tissue ears and noses are made of. Sometimes an implant is used instead of cartilage.)

Lori woke up in recovery feeling really groggy, but not in pain. "It just felt like pressure, I felt like a mummy with my head wrapped!" she says. A few minutes after awakening, she vomited suddenly. "No one had told me that I might do that," she says. "But it was only once."

Within a few hours she was ready to go home. "I spent the afternoon lying down," she says. "They had given me pain pills, but I only took one or two and never needed any more. It was much more like pressure than pain."

What she could see of her face looked swollen and bruised through the bandages, she says. "I looked awful. My best friend and her little sister came over to visit me the next day—her sister just stood there and stared at me and then said, 'I have to go' and left! When I looked in the mirror I could see why she was scared," Lori says.

Removing the cotton rolls packed inside her nose to prevent bleeding was the worst part because it hurt, she says. Seeing her new nose was a thrill even though it was hard to tell at first what it would finally look like. "But it was smaller!" she says.

Lori spent a normal summer after the first week, going to her job and spending time with her friends. The bruising faded and the swelling went down.

Lori liked her new nose but admits it was not exactly as she had pictured it. "I was hoping for a cute little model nose, but that wasn't realistic. It was still my nose, just smaller," she says. "But I am still happy with it. I would say my expectations basically were met. I've never regretted having the surgery, never been sorry at all."

While not everyone is as happy with surgery as Lori, she has some advice for teens who feel a part of their body is not attractive. "I would say if you truly believe something looks bad, go ahead and do it," she says. "There are people who are obsessed with their looks and maybe for them no amount of change will make them happy. But for people who really have something unattractive and who are realistic about it, I think it's OK. I think it can even be a healthy thing. I know I was a lot more confident when I started college. I felt better about myself. I think I was able to handle college better because I wasn't self-conscious and thinking about myself all the time."[1]

Lori's story shows that cosmetic surgery can be helpful when a person has something about his or her body that the person feels is really unattractive, if it is something that can be "fixed" with cosmetic surgery.

But there are questions: What does "unattractive" mean? When is something bad enough to justify surgery? When is a person old enough to make the decision to have cosmetic surgery? Is a teenager ready to take that responsibility? Can teenagers have realistic expectations? When is "young" too young?

There are no easy answers to these questions, and no one answer is right for every teen.

Controversy swirled around a teen in England, Jenna Franklin, when her parents let her have cosmetic surgery to enlarge her breasts for her sixteenth birthday. Their unusual gift made headlines in the British newspapers. The *Daily Express* said, "Jenna is pretty and intelligent. So why on earth is her mother buying breast implants for her sixteenth birthday?"[2]

Jenna says she started thinking about implants at age twelve. "Every other person you see on the television has had implants," she said. "If I want to be successful, I need

Before considering cosmetic surgery, teens need to carefully examine the issue from all angles.

to have them, too—and I do want to be successful, though I don't know at what at the moment."[3]

Her mother, Kay Franklin, felt she had made the right decision, saying that having larger breasts would boost her daughter's self-confidence. She herself has had several cosmetic procedures, including surgery on her nose and cheeks and liposuction (sucking out fat) on her hips.[4]

No matter what you think of Jenna and her parents' decision—there are people on both sides of the issue—it brings forward the pros and cons of teens having cosmetic surgery. Should Jenna have done it? Was she too young to make the decision? Was she too young for that type of surgery? There is no one right answer for every case.

Cosmetic surgery is a form of plastic surgery. In medical terms, plastic surgery involves altering, replacing, or restoring a part of the body to correct a structural or cosmetic defect. One type of plastic surgery is called reconstructive or corrective surgery. It is done to correct a birth defect or to repair damage from an accident, for example to correct a cleft lip. That type of surgery is considered medically necessary. In most cases, health insurance will pay for it. Cosmetic surgery is done to improve a person's appearance. It is not typically covered by health insurance.

In this book we will look at the pros and cons of cosmetic surgery for teens. We will explore why teens want surgery—good reasons, as well as some that may not be so good. We will also take a close look at the different types of procedures, including which ones are suitable for teens and which are not, and at what ages.

Kate's Story *continued*

eyes was like one big bruise. I had to be on a liquid diet for more than a week. I lost sixteen pounds."

At first she was not happy with how she looked. "It really freaked me out, my face looked so different!" she says. "I'd look in the mirror and cry. But when I had my senior pictures taken, I actually recognized myself—I had gotten used to looking different. I feel I look better now, but it took me two years to get to that point.

"Now I can chew and most of the pain in my jaw is gone. I have a chin like other people. I'm glad I had it done, but thinking about the amount of pain, I'm not sure I would do it again. I still don't really like my nose, and sometimes I think about having a real nose job, but then I think about the pain and I think, 'Do I not like it so much that I'm willing to go through all that just to fix something that is so minor?'

"I think you should really know who you are before you decide to have something like that done."[2]

were done on teens; in 2001, that percentage had more than tripled to 3½ percent.[3]

That number only includes the teens who are actually having cosmetic surgery. Even more are thinking about cosmetic surgery or would jump at the chance to do it if they could find a way.

One teen magazine, *Seabreeze*, did an online survey of three thousand girls. They published their results in January, 1999. A majority of the girls surveyed— 54 percent—said they would change one of their physical features if they had the chance.[4]

Another Internet survey, done by Seventeen magazine, had a larger sample. Four thousand teenagers, ages fourteen to eighteen, responded. Almost half said they were not happy with their bodies, and a third were thinking about some type of cosmetic surgery, most often breast implants or liposuction.[5]

Is such an obsession with the way they look normal for teens? Teenagers have always worried about their looks and spent a lot of time in front of mirrors. Part of growing up is learning who you are, and that includes how you look. Wanting to be your best, experimenting to find the most flattering clothes, makeup, and hairstyles, can all be part of building a healthy self-image.

But teens today face much stronger pressures to look good than in the past. Modern technology and the entertainment and fashion industries have changed the way we look at beauty.

In the 1950s, movie star Marilyn Monroe was considered the height of beauty. But by today's standards, with her round hips and slight belly, she would probably be considered too fat. Today's "beauty queens" are often stick slender but with large breasts, a combination not often found naturally. They often have tiny, pert noses

Teens today face a lot of pressure to look "perfect"—from the media, friends, and even themselves. However, before planning for cosmetic surgery, teens should wait until they are older to see if they still feel the same way.

and big, shiny lips. Their skin is usually perfect, without a single blemish.

"When young girls look at these beautiful women, what they don't get right away is that these women start beautiful," says Dr. Margaret Sullivan, a cultural psychologist. "They have experts making them up for several hours to look even more beautiful, and then the final photo is airbrushed or computer-enhanced so that any

Kim's Story

One night Kim and her high school boyfriend were walking along the side of a road. A bunch of guys in a car pulled over and shouted out the window, "Show us your fat boobs!"

Kim, who was at that time wearing a double D size bra, was used to comments like that. They hurt, but she had learned to ignore them.

That is what life was like through high school. When she went to college she gained a few pounds all over her body, as many freshmen do. She lost the weight, but it seemed to her that her breasts stayed at the larger size. "They became even more cumbersome," she says.

She began suffering constant back pain. A chiropractor told her nothing would really take care of the pain as long as the weight of her breasts pulled so hard on her back.

"I had talked about breast reduction surgery for years—I guess I didn't realize how much I talked about it until I started really researching it and my friends and family said, 'Finally! You've been talking about it for so long!'" Kim says.

Kim's Story *continued*

During her senior year of college, she decided the time had come. She scheduled her surgery for spring break. "Everything went very smoothly," she says. "My health insurance agreed to pay for it. I was out for about seven hours. I woke up bandaged completely; I had to stay in the hospital overnight. There were drains that had to be emptied for three days until they took them out. That was probably the most uncomfortable part. I didn't take that much pain medication."

Her bra size has now gone from a double D ("The doctor who measured me said I would have been wearing an E or F if they made them!" she laughs) to a C. "It's such a difference," she says. "My roommate is an artist. She did a plaster mold of my body before the surgery. Now when I look at it I can't believe that was me! My friends tell me I look much thinner even though only the top has changed; I'm more in proportion.

"It's been such a positive, good thing. I'm so happy to be rid of the problems."[11]

imperfection is removed. And so what's a poor girl to do? Go to your friendly plastic surgeon to try to emulate this totally unreal degree of beauty?"[6]

Airbrushing and computer enhancement refer to ways to "doctor" a photograph to remove any flaw. An enhanced photograph shows a "perfect person." The real person may not be nearly so perfect.

Cosmetic surgery on famous Hollywood stars used to be hush-hush. Stars and their doctors went to great lengths to keep surgical nips and tucks quiet. But today the stars are much more open about the surgery they have had, adding to the pressure on teens who want to look like them. Some examples: Janet Jackson admits that she had a rib removed to make her waist smaller; Lil' Kim, Toni Braxton, and Pam Anderson have all had breast implants. (Braxton and Anderson have also had their implants rupture or leak—a danger that will be discussed later in the book.)[7]

All this pressure to look "perfect" can cause teens to shudder when they look in the mirror and see someone they think is less than perfect looking back. Dr. Ann Kearney-Cooke, a scholar for the Partnership for Women's Health at Columbia University, analyzed the data from the *Seventeen* survey. She found that girls who are thinking about cosmetic surgery are also more likely to have eating disorders. They may also have problems such as low self-esteem and a feeling of disliking their bodies.[8]

"I would say that the media today has the most influence on kids," says Laura Gray, a psychotherapist who works with teenagers. "They will often say, 'I want to look like Kate Moss or Ally McBeal.' They will say flat-out that they know that's not realistic, but it's what they want. I think the message that kids are getting is that your value is equal to your appearance. If you are not completely perfect and attractive in every way, you don't count in this world."

Gray says pressure from friends is part of the picture. It is not so much pressure to have surgery, but to be perfect. It often takes the form of constantly talking about appearance, especially among girls. "They say things like, 'I wish I were that thin,' or 'her butt is too big' or 'I could never stand to look like that,'" she says. "Boys don't think they have a role in that, but they do. They often are the ones doing the teasing. A fair number of girls I see in therapy tell me about the comments about their appearance they hear in the hallway from boys, the clique dialogue they hear about other people, and things they hear said about themselves."[9]

Teens who are lonely, who do not have a lot of friends, or who do not have a boyfriend or girlfriend may be tempted to think that their social problems are all caused by their looks. They may begin to think that if they could just get rid of their big nose or have larger breasts they would be happy and popular and find romance. They do not realize that may not necessarily be true.

Parents, too, can contribute to the pressure to be perfect. Most parents love their kids just as they are, imperfections and all. But a few parents may want so much to have the perfect child that they pressure their child to have surgery to correct something that bothers them—even if it does not bother the teen.

In extreme cases, teens can develop a condition called body dysmorphic disorder (BDD). This is a disabling condition in which the person is obsessed with and very unhappy about some part of his or her body. Symptoms include spending hours on clothes or makeup to hide the body part the person thinks is flawed, constantly checking appearance in a mirror (or, the opposite, refusing to ever look in a mirror), constantly touching or measuring the "bad" feature, constantly thinking about how attractive other people are, or constantly comparing one's looks with other people's. People with BDD can be so anxious around other people that they will not go to social events because of worry over looks and may constantly ask other people for assurance that they look "normal." They may refuse to accept a cosmetic surgeon's opinion that surgery is not needed and seek more and more medical opinions.

Katherine Phillips, a psychiatrist at Brown University, says in her book, *The Broken Mirror*, that 5 million Americans have BDD. But she admits that it can be hard to separate BDD from normal concerns about appearance.[10]

In light of all these pressures, should teenagers have cosmetic surgery? It is not possible to give a yes-or-no answer to that question. It depends on many factors: emotional and physical maturity, the reason for wanting the surgery, and how realistic the person's expectations are.

3

The Pros and Cons of Cosmetic Surgery for Teens

There is no easy answer to the question of whether or not teenagers should have cosmetic surgery. Different doctors have different opinions.

"I think that [cosmetic surgery for teens] borders on the unethical," said John Grossman, a plastic surgeon in Beverly Hills, California. "It's taking advantage of the natural inclination of adolescents and of parents who unfortunately have more money than good sense."[1]

Another doctor has a different opinion. "Being called 'Dumbo' because his ears stick out or 'Pinocchio' if her nose is too big can crush a youngster's sense of self-esteem before it has a chance to solidify. . . . The goal of cosmetic surgery, particularly among young people, is to make people look 'normal' so they will feel more comfortable with themselves. Indeed, getting teased or feeling self-conscious about a physical feature might interfere with a young person's character development and ability to learn," says Arthur Perry, a cosmetic surgeon and co-author of a book on cosmetic surgery.[2] Not all doctors and counselors who work with youth would agree with him, but many would.

The American Society of Plastic Surgeons, the professional organization that cosmetic surgeons belong to, does not have a position on cosmetic surgery for teens. Instead, it tells members to think about each individual case carefully before deciding whether or not to do surgery.

Here are the factors the society tells members to weigh:

1. *Is it the teen that wants the surgery?* Teens need support from their parents, but it must be the teen who really wants the surgery, not the parents.

2. *Does the teen have realistic goals?* He or she must know the benefits and the limitations of surgery and not think it will mean perfection or take away all of life's problems.

3. *Is the teen mature enough to make this decision?* The teen has to be able to weigh the pros and cons and be willing to put up with any pain, discomfort, or temporary disfigurement. And he or she must be able to do the needed care after the surgery.[3]

The "Pro" Side: Reasons to Have Cosmetic Surgery

Michelle could not see her pretty eyes and smile because when she looked in a mirror, all she could see was her nose. "I had a hump on my nose. Every time I looked at my profile, it made me feel really bad about myself. I didn't want to feel that way for the rest of my life," she says. So she had her nose "done." The operation cost $3,500 in 1999, but when it was over, she had the straight nose she had always wanted. Now she says her new nose has given her confidence. "I definitely feel more comfortable with myself," she says. "But even though you fix the outside, your inside is still the same. That's what matters the most—having a good personality and a good heart."[4] Yet, she still felt strongly enough about her nose to have it fixed.

"There is no question that teens are susceptible to peer pressure; another big factor is the media," says Dr. David Larson, a cosmetic surgeon and chairman of the department of plastic surgery at the Medical College of Wisconsin. "Kids this age are very concerned about their bodies and their self images; they tend to focus on the areas they see as a problem. They don't focus on their strengths—their pretty skin or beautiful eyes. Instead, when they look in the mirror, they see only the parts of the body that bother them—a little extra weight around the hips or a nose or ears that stick out. They tend to zero in on that negative part, ignoring the positives. They look at their basket as 5 percent empty instead of 95 percent full."[5]

Because of that focus, he says, teens can have problems with self-confidence and self-esteem if they have a feature they think is unattractive. Cosmetic surgery, he says, can help.

"If the surgeon chooses the right operation for the right patient, he or she will have a happy patient," he says. "There's no question that it can improve self-esteem and self-image. If the surgery is really indicated, I can give the teen a more positive view of themselves, which will lead to a better interaction with the world around them."[6]

Psychotherapist Laura Gray agrees that in some circumstances, cosmetic surgery can be a positive. "If the teasing is so awful that the teen can't function in school, can't concentrate on school work, can't participate in sports without it becoming an issue, then I think cosmetic surgery might be warranted," she says. "That would be my benchmark—if the person is not able to get successfully through adolescence and become a healthy, functioning adult because of the problem. Absolutely, you can increase self-esteem, but I think most kids need some sort of guidance or therapy at the same time so they don't think they are getting this magical fix and once the surgery is done everything is going to be fine."[7]

Samantha was a teen who had large, heavy breasts. She had breast reduction surgery in her early teens. She is pleased with the result. Clothes fit better; she now owns more than the three shirts that fit before the surgery. "No one looks at me like I'm a freak anymore. But, after all, I just got smaller boobs. I'm still the same person," she says.[8]

Better self-image and greater acceptance by peer groups can be two big benefits to having cosmetic surgery. But the picture is not all positive. There are risks to such surgery also.

The "Con" Side: Reasons Not to Have Cosmetic Surgery

Mary was only sixteen when she had breast implants put in to make her breasts larger. She says she did it to please her mother. But she says the implants have brought a lot of physical and emotional problems. "Sometimes they'll heat up and they'll burn, they'll pinch," she said in a television interview. "I feel I was a child [when she had the implants]; I feel that should never be done to any child. I feel it teaches the wrong things. We need to teach and love children. I don't think putting breast implants in a child does that."[9]

There are two kinds of risks in having cosmetic surgery: physical risks and psychological risks.

Physical risks

Cosmetic surgery always requires an anesthetic. Sometimes a general anesthetic that puts a person "out" is used and sometimes a local anesthetic that numbs the area is used. It always means cutting and stitching. There are risks involved in all of those things, says Dr. Larson. Reactions to anesthetics are rare, but they can happen. Allergic responses can cause heart rhythm or breathing problems. Heavy bleeding is also rare, but it can happen. Wounds can become infected. Stitches can pull out. Healing can be slow, especially in teens who smoke.[10]

More often, the problem may be that the result of the operation is not 100 percent perfect. "After the surgery people can become very critical of little bumps that others can't see but they can feel," Dr. Larson says. "Sometimes the surgeon will have to do a little revision to make the result better. I don't call that a complication, but it is an unexpected result of the surgery."

There will always be some pain and downtime after surgery. Procedures have improved over the last few years, so discomfort and time out of school or work are much less now than years ago. But still, no one should expect to have surgery in the morning and go out with friends that night.

"If I do surgery on Thursday or Friday, I will want the person to take off the next week. The following week they can be pretty much back at full tilt except for carrying heavy books and backpacks for a few weeks," Dr. Larson says. "Most surgeries do require some pain medication; there is some discomfort. But a person probably wouldn't be on pain medication constantly for more than a week or so."

Very rarely, a cosmetic surgery can be "botched" so that the person comes out with severe scars or distortion of the feature that was operated on. To help avoid that risk, it is important to choose a qualified, experienced surgeon.

Psychological risks

The biggest psychological risk is that a teen will put all of his or her hopes into this operation. Once it is done, he or she thinks, life will be perfect. "I will be the most popular person in my class, I will get a great new boyfriend or girlfriend, I will always be happy, and everything will be wonderful," a teen may think. That person is not living in reality.

"There has to be an education process; the teen has to learn what to expect from the operation," says Dr. Larson. "I talk to every teenager alone at some point, and with his or her parents. I need to identify a level of maturity in the person. There are some very mature fifteen-year-olds and some very immature eighteen-year-olds. I need to identify the person's expectations. What do you want? What are you looking for?"

Teens who do not have that basic understanding, whose expectations are out of line with reality, will not be happy with the cosmetic surgery no matter how good it looks, says Laura Gray. "How do you handle disappointment when you didn't get what you thought you were going to get? Often kids have this really big fantasy in their heads about how life is going to be—and then it's not. Or they don't look like they thought they would after the surgery. Those kids need a lot of help and guidance from their parents or, if it is really bad, from a professional to cope."[11]

An ethical cosmetic surgeon will not do cosmetic surgery on just any teenager who asks for it. There are some red flags that should make a cosmetic surgeon turn down a teen's request.

1. The person has an unrealistic expectation of what the surgery can do physically—a teen needs to realize he or she will not look like a movie star.

Teens and parents need to meet with the plastic surgeon to get full information on any cosmetic procedure. At the same time, a good doctor should be watching a teen closely to see if the teen is really a good candidate for the surgery.

2. The person has an unrealistic expectation of how much life will improve after the surgery. "Often kids are looking for happiness and I don't know that you can get that through surgery," Laura Gray says.

3. The person expects that all peer pressure and teasing will stop once the operation is done.

4. The person is clinically depressed or has other signs of mental illness.

5. The person abuses drugs or alcohol.

6. The person seems obsessed with perfection.

7. The person has wide mood swings, or changes his or her mind constantly on things like fashions or hairstyles.

8. The teen's parents seem to be the ones who want the surgery; the teen seems not to care very much.[12]

"I think there are definitely times when cosmetic surgery is warranted, but I also think there are teens who are feeding into peer pressure for appearance," Gray says. "Most adults I know are successful because they've been handed things that aren't perfect and they have to figure out how to get around that. Too often we want to run in and rescue teenagers and the message we send is, 'I don't think you can handle it.' But they can. You have to give them time to see what they can do."[13]

She points out that being physically perfect does not necessarily mean a having perfect, happy life. "Look at what some of the Hollywood types and models are doing today," she says. "Some of them are going into volunteer work and other things that make a difference. I think the statement they are trying to send is that perfect appearance isn't all what it's cracked up to be—it can be a very meaningless existence. I'd like to see more kids get the message that looking good isn't everything."

4

The Procedures and How They Are Done

The world of cosmetic surgery procedures is somewhat different for teens compared to adults. Some procedures are only done for adults—there are not, after all, many teens who need a face-lift.

Other procedures are done for both teens and adults, but there may be more factors to consider when doing them on teens. Teen cosmetic surgery is often done to make a body part smaller or bigger. But not every procedure is a good idea for all ages, and some can be done earlier than others.

Rhinoplasty

According the American Society of Plastic Surgeons, the most popular cosmetic surgery for teens—about one third of all teen surgeries—is nose reshaping, or rhinoplasty.[1] *Rhino* refers to the nose, and *plasty* means to improve

Choosing a Surgeon

Any doctor who has graduated from medical school and qualified for a physician's license can be called a cosmetic surgeon, even if he or she did not specialize in that area. It is important to find a surgeon who has specialized in cosmetic surgery and who has experience in that field. Here are some questions to ask:

- Is the doctor accredited by the American Board of Plastic Surgery? People considering surgery can get information from the Plastic Surgery Information Service or the American Society of Plastic Surgeons Web site.

- Does the surgeon have privileges (is allowed to operate) at an accredited hospital? If the surgeon works from a day-surgery clinic, is it accredited by the American Association for Accreditation of Ambulatory Surgery Facilities? Ask if the facility has lifesaving equipment in case it is needed.

- Is the person who gives the anesthetic accredited? Are the people who care for patients registered nurses?

- Does the surgeon have satisfied patients? Ask for references. Do not choose a surgeon just because he or she has been quoted in the media or because of an advertisement in a magazine.[2]

Many cosmetic procedures today are done at freestanding cosmetic day surgery centers. Before having a procedure done at such a place, it is important to make sure they have lifesaving equipment in case an emergency arises.

through plastic surgery. The nose usually keeps growing until about age fifteen to seventeen for girls and about sixteen to eighteen for boys. Rhinoplasty normally is not done until growth stops, unless there is a good reason to do it earlier.[3]

Dr. Tracy McCall is a plastic surgeon who works with teens in her practice. Some teens she sees have broken noses that need to be straightened. But more often they come because their nose has a bump they do not like or because they feel their nose is too big or crooked. Surgery to correct those problems, she explains, is done using incisions on the inside of the nose. The only outside incision is likely to be underneath the nose where it is not easily seen.[4]

There are some risks in rhinoplasty. "You are breaking bones or shaving down a bump a little," she explains. "The bones need to touch in the middle again, otherwise it's like cutting the top off a house—there can be pieces of wall sticking out. You have to be careful to get the smoothness back. And, if you take out too much, the cartilage can collapse."

She tells her patients that perfection is not possible. "Most people's noses are not exactly the same on both sides," she points out. "That's normal. Trying to make the nose a carbon copy on both sides would be making it a little abnormal."

Sometimes the nose does not turn out exactly as the patient wanted it to look. "I tell patients not to try to look like a certain movie star," she says. "You don't want to have the same nose on everybody's face. Everyone is supposed to look different. You want the nose that looks right for your face."

She recommends that her patients wait for surgery until after their noses have stopped growing. "I want to make sure the nose is fully developed," she says. "I'd probably wait until at least age sixteen, or even a little later, unless there was a bad fracture."

Sometimes, in case of injury or when the person has trouble breathing because of the shape of the nose, rhinoplasty may be medical rather than just cosmetic. In that case, health insurance may pay for part or all of the operation.[5]

Chin Implants

Many teens who have their noses made smaller have their chins made a little bigger at the same time to make the face look more balanced. That can be done using bone removed from the nose or chin or an implant, Dr. McCall says.[6]

"You pull the lower lip out and make a small incision on the inside," she explains. "You pull up the tissue and place the implant inside. Everything is sewn back together and there it stays." There is small risk of the implant being rejected or moving out of place.

She points out that chin implants, like nose reshaping, should not be done until the jawbone stops growing. It is also important, she says, to look at how the teeth fit together. "If the problem is just a small chin, then an implant can correct it," she says. "But in some people the teeth don't fit together properly; that has to be corrected before you put in the implant." As with the nose, she prefers to wait to do a chin implant until the patient is age sixteen or older.

Breast Reduction

It may seem that having breasts made bigger would be the more popular operation; actually, having them made smaller is done more often on teenagers.[7] Many people are surprised to learn that the operation is done on males as well as females.

In girls, it may be that breast development begins too early or that the breasts grow so large that they are uncomfortable. Surgery is usually not done until the breasts have stopped developing (about age sixteen). But in rare cases girls may develop very large breasts as early as age eleven or twelve. "In those cases, breast reduction can be done early, as soon as age twelve," says Dr. McCall. "That has to be an individual decision for each patient."[8]

Girls who have very large breasts can be embarrassed and stared at in public. Sometimes people make unkind remarks that can be very hurtful. Life can become miserable. There can also be physical problems. "Large breasts can cause back and neck pain," Dr. McCall says. "Bra straps can cut deep grooves in the shoulders. The breasts can hurt or have a rash underneath." She points out that making large breasts that are causing problems smaller is often not cosmetic surgery, but medically necessary. Health insurance often will pay for it.

Males can also develop breast tissue. About half of all males will have some breast development as they become teenagers. In most cases it will go away on its own. If it does not, it can be very embarrassing for a boy. There are many reasons why it can happen, including hormone problems or being overweight. Many teens do not know that smoking pot can increase breast tissue in males.

Dr. McCall points out that it is important for a boy to have a medical exam to find out what is causing the breast enlargement before anything is done. If hormones and other factors are normal, the extra breast tissue can be removed surgically. Some insurance companies pay for this procedure and some do not.

"The way breast reduction is done is very different for boys and girls," she says. "In women you are removing some of the tissue. You basically take the breast apart and then fold it back together to form a more normal breast— it's almost like origami using human tissue!

"In a boy, you take away all of the breast. You try to make it as smooth with the rest of the chest as you can. If the breast isn't too big, you might be able to do it with liposuction [removing the fat with a vacuum device]. In other cases you may have to remove a little saucer of fat tissue along with the liposuction."

In a girl, it is important to try to keep a normal nipple so she will be able to breast-feed a baby later in life, Dr. McCall says. "We try to keep the nipple attached on a stalk of tissue although sometimes we have to take it off and put it back on as a skin graft," she explains. "Not everyone will be able to breast-feed after this surgery, but there is a chance." Many teens prefer to think about today rather than the future, but the risk of not being able to breast-feed when they want to is something teenage girls must think about before deciding on breast reduction.

Males need to wear a tight elastic band around their chest for a month or two after the surgery to support the area. Females will need to wear a good support bra.

Sometimes, rather than needing to have both breasts reduced, the problem is that one breast is a different size or shape than the other. That can be corrected by making one smaller, one larger, or both.

There are some risks in breast reduction surgery, Dr. McCall says. There will be scars; that cannot be avoided. In women, the scars are hidden under the breasts and around the nipple. In males, the doctor will try to limit the scar to around the nipple. However, sometimes the scars can be very noticeable. Females can lose nipple function; the nipple itself can be lost and have to be rebuilt artificially. The new breasts may not be exactly the same size. If the person later gains a lot of weight, the breasts can become too big again.

Breast Augmentation

Breasts can be made larger by putting in an implant. Breast implants are silicone shells filled with a saltwater solution called saline. They used to be filled with silicone gel, but because of reports of health problems from the silicone (which were never completely proved) saline is now used. Silicone implants may be allowed again in the future.

The surgery is usually done under general anesthetic. The surgeon makes an incision either under the breast, around the areola (the circle of dark skin around the nipple), or in the armpit. He or she will lift the tissue to create a pocket, either behind the breast tissue or under the chest wall muscle. The implants are put into that pocket, centered under the nipples.[9]

"I do not like to see young girls asking for breast augmentation," says Dr. McCall. "They are still developing, still changing. Most importantly, their idea of what is important is still changing. If you are under sixteen and you come to me, I'll tell you to wait until you are older. There could be an odd exception to the rule, but I want my patients to be at least eighteen."[10]

There are risks in augmentation, she points out. "You are putting in a foreign body. The implants can pop and deflate (the body absorbs the solution). Then it's gone and you have to have it replaced. The body can also form a capsule of scar tissue around the implant and that can constrict so the breast becomes hard and deformed."

She is concerned about the effect of having breast implants over a lifetime when they are put in at a young age. "If you have this done when you are sixteen you can expect to live sixty or seventy years with the implant," she points out. "I don't think the implants will last that long; at some time you will probably need more surgery to replace them."

A surgeon will try not to harm the nipple while doing the surgery. Most of the time breast-feeding will not be affected by an implant. But there is some risk of losing sensation in the nipples. Also, implants can get in the way of a mammogram, an X-ray used to find breast cancer. A woman who has them will need to find a doctor who knows how to do mammograms on breasts with implants. Mammograms are usually done starting at age forty.[11]

Liposuction

In liposuction, the doctor makes a small incision in the skin, usually using a general anesthetic. He or she then puts the end of a hollow tube, called a cannula, into the fat layer underneath the skin. It is attached to a machine that creates a strong vacuum. The doctor moves the cannula through the fat layers under the skin, breaking up the fat and sucking it out. Sometimes more than one incision is needed. The patient will need to wear a tight elastic dressing for several weeks while things heal.[12]

"Liposuction is not a weight-loss technique," Dr. McCall states. "The most fat you can take out at one time is only a few pounds. It won't help someone who is fifty pounds overweight."[13]

Liposuction is designed for an isolated spot, such as the side of the thigh or the abdomen where fat tends to stick (sometimes exercise and dieting will not make such fat deposits go away). But, it is not meant for all-over weight loss. "Liposuction is really more about smoothing and contouring the body than losing weight," she says. "If someone came to me and said, 'I want to go from size twelve jeans to size six,' I would say, 'Go on a diet!'"

She points out that there are risks in liposuction that many people do not realize. "While you are sucking out fat, you are also sucking out fluids and disrupting the body's fluid balance," she says. "You have to be careful with that. If you give the person too much replacement fluid, they can

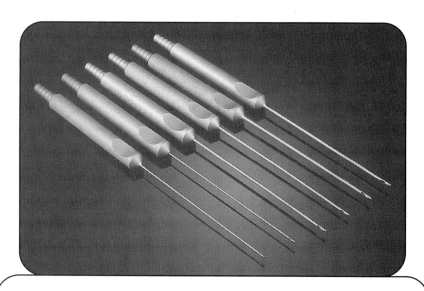

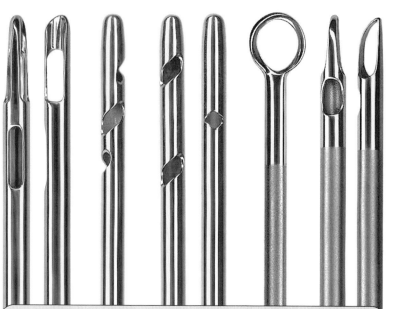

These cannulas are used in liposuction. They are inserted under the skin to suck fat out.

swell up so much their heart can't handle it. People can die from liposuction!" A skilled surgeon can judge how much fluid the patient needs and not overdo the replacement.

Dr. McCall would not normally consider doing any liposuction on someone under the age of sixteen. "That's the minimum unless someone had a very abnormal fat deposit," she says.

Liposuction is not always permanent, she points out. "The fat may not come back in just the same spot, but if you don't change your eating habits, fat will come back all over and the part you had liposuctioned will get bigger too."

Sometimes, in very overweight people, there will be loose skin left hanging after the fat has been sucked out. That might mean another procedure, sometimes called a "tummy tuck," to remove the loose skin. That is not often needed on a teenager because the skin is still very elastic. "A better answer is weight loss," Dr. McCall says.

"Ear Pinning"

Called otoplasty (*oto* refers to the ear and *plasty* means to improve by plastic surgery), this surgery is often done on children whose ears stick out. Children with large ears that do not lie close to the head are often teased. Being called "Dumbo" or "flap ears" can cause a great deal of emotional pain.

To make the ear lie flatter against the head, the doctor makes an incision in the back of the ear and removes a wedge of cartilage. In smaller ears, the cartilage may not have to be taken out; just cutting into it may be enough to bring the ear closer to the head.[14]

"This surgery is really quite common in kids," says Dr. McCall.[15] She points out that it is usually done around the age of six, but it can be done a little earlier if necessary.

The child has to be willing to wear a band, like a sweatband, around the ears for six weeks or so after the surgery.

The biggest risk is that the operation might not work well enough and the ears still stick out too much, she says. If the surgery is not done carefully, the shape of the ear may be abnormal. But those risks are very small. "This operation is one that is fine to do with teenagers also," she says.

Lip, Cheekbone, or Muscle Enlargement

This group of cosmetic surgery procedures is much less common, especially among teenagers. While people in the entertainment and fashion industry may have their lips and cheekbones enlarged with injections of fat or small implants, not many teenagers are having such procedures.

"Would I do those things in a teenager? No, I would not," says Dr. McCall. "Having big lips, just like having big breasts, will not make people like you." She points out that lip injections can make the lips swell too much or they can turn out different sizes. The fat will gradually be absorbed and they will shrink back down. She would do cheekbone implants only for cases in which the sides of the face did not develop correctly and one side was smaller than the other.

She points out that muscle implants are beginning to be popular with teenage boys who are into bodybuilding. Small "artificial muscles" can be put into the chest wall or into arms or legs to make them look more muscular. Some people, looking for a more rounded shape, are getting implants for their buttocks. Dr. McCall would not recommend these procedures for teens. "Teen's bodies are changing, so is their idea of what the body should look like," she says. "This is something that has to be well thought out and should only be done on adults, if then."

She points out there is a risk of infection and of the implant coming out of the body. "I had one patient who had butt implants put in in another country," she recalls. "One implant worked its way out of the incision. I had to take it out and clean everything out. Then she was lopsided, so she had to have another implant." An implant can be removed if the person no longer wants it.

Skin Improvement

Teenagers and acne seem to go together. Untreated, skin flare-ups can lead to scars, both on the surface as well as deeper scars that look like someone stabbed the skin with an ice pick.

The "big three H's" that cause acne are hormones, hygiene, and heredity. According to Michelle Bonness, M.D., a plastic surgeon, the problem starts with excess oil. "The pores get clogged, bacteria are trapped, an infection results—that is acne," she explains. Washing affected skin frequently and using over-the-counter products can help.

If the acne is severe, a dermatologist (a skin doctor) can prescribe antibiotics or a drug called Accutane® to dry up the oil and stop the infection. "There is also a brand-new type of laser to treat active acne; it kills the bacteria," Dr. Bonness says. This treatment is usually covered by insurance.

If the acne causes scars, a plastic surgeon has several different options to treat them. Surface scars can be treated with a laser. "Some of the lasers work by taking off the top layer of skin," Dr. Bonness says. "Some newer lasers work by stimulating the deeper skin to fill in the scars."

For deeper scars, plastic surgeons can use a procedure called dermabrasion, which literally sands off the scars. Classic dermabrasion is done with a machine that looks

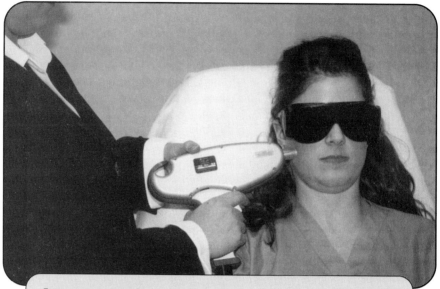

Laser treatment for acne is an expensive procedure that does not guarantee perfect skin.

like something you would find in someone's garage, explains Dr. Bonness. "A little metal bit spins around at high speed and takes off several layers of skin." Often this form of dermabrasion is used together with a laser; the dermabrasion works on the edges of the scars and the laser does the rest.

Both laser and classic dermabrasion are done in an operating room under anesthetic. Afterwards the skin is raw much like a burn; it must be covered with bandages for five days and treated with ointment for another week because there is a risk of infection. The skin will stay pink for many weeks and will be easily sunburned. There is a risk of blotchy skin color later.

A second, milder form of dermabrasion can be done in the doctor's office. It uses sand blown at high speed against the skin, sanding off the scars. This form does not result in downtime, but it only works on more superficial scars.

Deep "ice pick" scars cannot be removed by any of these means; they are usually cut out, leaving behind a much smaller scar.

Laser and classic dermabrasion are very expensive procedures because they require an operating room and anesthetic. In most cases insurance will not pay because scars are considered a cosmetic problem. Figure the cost at thousands, not hundreds, of dollars.

None of these procedures can promise perfect, smooth skin, Dr. Bonness says. "But they can greatly improve it."[16]

5

Making the Decision

Danielle did not like her thighs. "I was very self-conscious about my shape," she says. "I had pouches on the sides of my thighs. When I looked at myself, I didn't think I looked normal compared to everyone else."[1]

At age nineteen, Danielle had liposuction to remove the fat deposits on the outside of her thighs. Her parents paid the four-thousand-dollar bill.[2]

Danielle's surgery illustrates two points about cosmetic surgery for teenagers: In most cases the surgery is not medically necessary, and it costs a lot of money. There are other points to consider: The teen's life may or may not change after the surgery, and all surgery carries some risk.

How should a teenager thinking about cosmetic surgery make the decision to either go ahead or to say, "No, this is not right for me?"

Think of using a scale that has two baskets balanced on a center pole. Into one of the baskets go all the benefits that would likely result from having the surgery:

- feeling better about improved appearance
- having better self-esteem and confidence
- perhaps being more comfortable physically

Into the other basket go all the risks:

- bleeding, infection, reaction to the anesthetic
- not looking absolutely perfect after it is done
- finding life does not change and all problems do not disappear after surgery
- realizing after surgery that there is no such thing as a miracle short-cut to making life better—including changing one's appearance
- paying the bill

Only when the benefit side of the scale outweighs the risk side is surgery a good idea.

Here are some questions to ask while thinking about the decision:

How necessary is this surgery? A teenager with a truly unattractive feature such as a huge nose or ears that stick out is in a different place than one who has a tiny bump on the nose or thighs that are not stick-slender. A teen thinking about surgery should try to honestly evaluate how bad the offending feature really is. Is there constant, cruel teasing, or just someone who once said, "Hey, bump-nose, how's it going?" Do other people really see nothing but your nose? Or are you so obsessed that you can see nothing else when everyone else barely notices?

Asking friends what they think can be useful. If most of them agree that the offending feature is really bad, weigh that in the decision. But if most of them say, "Are you kidding—you are going to have surgery on that little bump?" listen to them. However, while friends' opinions can be useful, they should never be the only basis for deciding; remember, they may not be completely honest and may not be mature enough to give a valid opinion.

How realistic are my expectations? A teen considering surgery needs to shine the light of truth on what he or she expects to happen after it is done. Do you expect to look like a movie star or a model? Do you think you will finally get a boyfriend or girlfriend? Do you think the cloud of depression that has been around you will suddenly lift? Do you think life will be perfect once your nose is smaller or your breasts bigger? None of those things is likely to be true.

Am I mature enough to make this decision? Every teen likes to think he or she is much more mature and responsible than the average teen. It is very hard to weigh your own maturity, but you must try. Teens who have to be constantly told what to do may not be mature enough to make this decision yet. And remember, people feel differently about how they look as they get older; it may be worthwhile to wait a few years and see if you still feel the same way about your appearance.

Have I talked to informed adults? Teens thinking about cosmetic surgery need to talk to adults who know them and who know something about the procedure. Parents, a trusted adult friend, a school nurse, or a guidance counselor can all be good sources of information. After getting an opinion from one plastic surgeon, it can be a good idea to get a second opinion from another surgeon. There are books on cosmetic surgery and a great deal of

Talking to a trusted adult, like a parent, can help guide a teen to the right decision.

information on the Internet. Research is an important part of the decision.

Do I really understand all the risks? Teens thinking about cosmetic surgery need to understand the risks of anesthetics, bleeding, and infection. They need to know how much pain, swelling, and downtime to expect and be willing to cope with all of that. They should realize that while some people have a high pain tolerance and do not find cosmetic surgery too painful, there are others who find the pain very intense and long lasting. They need to understand what kind of care they will have to do right after the surgery—keeping incisions clean, wearing any necessary elastic bandages—and be willing to take the time to do it right.

How will I pay for it? Cosmetic surgery is not cheap. In most cases health insurance will not pay for it. Teens thinking about surgery need to find out exactly what it will cost. Costs vary in different parts of the country and go up every year, but procedures will cost thousands of dollars. Remember, the surgeon's fee is only one part; the hospital or clinic and the person who gives the anesthetic will also send a bill. Are your parents willing to foot the bill? If not, do you have enough money from a job or gifts to pay for it? Can you afford both surgery and the other things you want such as a car? What is most important? "I had one girl who worked at a fast-food job after school for months and months [to pay for surgery]. Another gave me fifty dollars a month for years to get breast implants," said one plastic surgeon.[3] Are you willing to do that? If you have a job, before making the decision it would be wise to find out the exact cost of the surgery, divide it by twelve or twenty-four or even thirty-six (depending on how many years it will take to pay the bill) to find the monthly cost. Then subtract that from your monthly paycheck to find out how much will be left after the payment.

Another tool to help in making the decision is the specialized computer many cosmetic surgeons now have that can take a picture of a person and digitally change it to show what he or she will look like after the surgery. Dr. Larson uses such a computer with his patients. "I can do the imaging and give them before and after pictures," he says. "It works the best on facial issues. It doesn't work as well for breasts."[4]

Some teens who go through this honest assessment process may decide that cosmetic surgery is not for them,

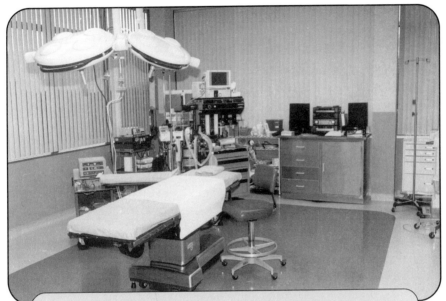

Cosmetic surgery is done in a complete operating room. This adds to the cost of the surgery, since the patient has to pay for the surgeon as well as for the room and the doctor giving the anesthetic.

or, at least, not at the present time. Surgery, after all, is not a one-time thing. Deciding not to do it now does not mean that it cannot be done in the future.

Other teens may, after weighing the pros and cons, decide that surgery is right for them. Many teens who go ahead with a cosmetic procedure are very pleased with the results and are glad they had it done.

"It's all about how you define the surgery and what it means to you," says Laura Gray. "It's about what you are looking for and if it is something that can be had through a physical change. I think there are times when it is warranted, but I also think teens have to be very careful that they are not just buying into the social value of appearance."[5]

This is not a decision to be made lightly but one to make only after careful thought, research, and weighing of all the factors. Only then can a teenager be sure he or she has made the best decision.

Living With What is Not "Perfect"

Cosmetic surgery is not the only answer for a part of the body that is not perfect. There are ways to deal with imperfection other than changing the body. Some suggestions adapted from a school program on building self-esteem:

- Remember that bodies change very fast during the teen years; the average girl will grow ten inches and gain thirty pounds from puberty to age eighteen. Sometimes just waiting will solve a problem—a nose may seem smaller when the whole face grows larger; breasts can still develop even after age eighteen.

- Body image is more than just body parts. Good hygiene, flattering clothes and makeup, and a warm, caring personality are more important to how other people see someone than perfect noses or slim thighs.

- Ideal beauty is an individual thing, not just what the fashion and entertainment worlds push as "beautiful."[6]

Chapter Notes

Chapter 1. Lori's Story
1. Personal interview with "Lori," January 17, 2002.
2. Quoted in C. Health, January 9, 2001, <http://www.canoe.ca/LifewiseFamilyTuesday01/0109_implants_ap.html> (January 13, 2001).
3. Ibid.
4. Ibid.

Chapter 2. Why Do Teenagers Consider Cosmetic Surgery?
1. Telephone interview with Kate, March 7, 2002.
2. Statistics from American Society for Aesthetic Plastic Surgery, n.d., <http://www.surgery.org/consumer_tips.html> (December 30, 2002).
3. Ibid.
4. Quoted in Genevieve Belfiglio, "Teens and Plastic Surgery: Too Young to Seek Perfection?" n.d., <http://www.CBSHealthwatch.com> (September 13, 2001).
5. Paula Gray Hunker, "Pressure to be Perfect," *Insight on the News*, vol. 16, issue 10, March 13, 2000, p. 29; Mary Powers, "Face Off: Teen-agers and Plastic Surgery May Not be the Greatest Mix," *Abilene Reporter-News*, Texnews/E.W. Scripps Publications, September 15, 2000, <http://www.reporternews.com> (September 13, 2001).
6. Quoted in Tracee Worley, "The Price of Beauty," KRON-TV, aired September 23, 1997, <http://www.firstcut.com/9717/nl.html> (September 13, 2001).
7. Jessica Bublitz and the Jump staff, "Body Alteration: Is It Worth It?" *The Milwaukee Journal Sentinel*, January 22, 2001, p. 4E.
8. Quoted in Genevieve Belfiglio, "Teens and Plastic Surgery: Too Young to Seek Perfection?" n.d., <http://www.CBSHealthwatch.com> (September 13, 2001).

9. Personal interview with Laura Gray, R.N., M.S.N., December 21, 2001.

10. Diana Zuckerman, Ph.D., "Ask Our Experts," Talksurgery.com, n.d., <http://www.talksurgery.com/consumer/articles/> (September 13, 2001); Diagnostic and Statistical Manual of Mental Disorders, 4th ed. (Washington, D.C.: American Psychiatric Association, 1994), pp. 466–468.

11. Telephone interview with Kim, March 27, 2002.

Chapter 3. The Pros and Cons of Cosmetic Surgery for Teens

1. Quoted in Michel Moutot, "Doctors Speak Out Against Performing Plastic Surgery on U.S. Teens," *Outsource*, distributed by the French News Wire Service, April 9, 2000, <http://www.beautifulme.com/today_french.html> (September 13, 2001).

2. Arthur Perry, M.D. and Robin Levinson, *Are You Considering Cosmetic Surgery?* (New York: Avon Books, 1997), pp. 197–198.

3. Adapted from "Plastic Surgery Briefing: Plastic Surgery for Teenagers," brochure from the American Society of Plastic Surgeons, n.d., <http://www.plasticsurgery.org/mediactr/teenbrief.html> (September 17, 2002).

4. Quoted in Karen Fanning, "Perfectly Plastic?" *Scholastic Choices*, March 2001, vol. 16, issue 6, p. 20.

5. Telephone interview with David Larson, M.D., December 14, 2001.

6. Ibid.

7. Personal interview with Laura Gray, R.N., M.S.N., December 21, 2001.

8. Quoted in Genevieve Belfiglio, "Teens and Plastic Surgery: Too Young to Seek Perfection?" n.d., <http://www.CBSHealthwatch.com> (September 13, 2001).

9. "Cosmetic Consent," KRON-TV, aired September 23, 1997, <http://www.kron.com/nc4/healthbeat/stories/cosmetic_consent.html> (September 17, 2001).

10. Telephone interview with David Larson, M.D., December 14, 2001.

11. Personal interview with Laura Gray, R.N., M.S.N., December 21, 2001.

12. Adapted from "Plastic Surgery Briefing: Plastic Surgery for Teenagers," brochure from the American Society of Plastic Surgeons, n.d., <http://www.plasticsurgery.org/mediactr/teenbrief.html> (September 17, 2002); "Should Teens Have Plastic Surgery?" *USA Today Magazine*, January 1992, vol. 120, issue 2560, p. 6; Telephone interview with David Larson, M.D., December 14, 2001.

13. Personal interview with Laura Gray, R.N., M.S.N., December 21, 2001.

Chapter 4. The Procedures and How They Are Done

1. Adapted from Kawanza Griffin, "Cosmetic Surgery: How to Pick the Right Surgeon," *The Milwaukee Journal-Sentinel*, May 15, 2000, p. 4G.

2. "Plastic Surgery Briefing: Plastic Surgery for Teenagers," brochure from the American Society of Plastic Surgeons, n.d., <http://www.plasticsurgery.org/mediactr/teenbrief.html> (September 17, 2002).

3. Josleen Wilson, *The American Society of Plastic and Reconstructive Surgeons' Guide to Cosmetic Surgery* (New York: Simon and Schuster, 1992), p. 90.

4. Personal interview with Tracy E. McCall, M.D., February 1, 2001.

5. "Plastic Surgery Briefing: Plastic Surgery for Teenagers," brochure from the American Society of Plastic Surgeons, n.d., <http://www.plasticsurgery.org/mediactr/teenbrief.html> (September 17, 2002).

6. Personal interview with Tracy E. McCall, M.D., February 1, 2001.

7. "Plastic Surgery Briefing: Plastic Surgery for Teenagers," brochure from the American Society of Plastic Surgeons, n.d., <http://www.plasticsurgery.org/mediactr/teenbrief.html> (September 17, 2002).

8. Personal interview with Tracy E. McCall, M.D., February 1, 2001.

9. "Breast Augmentation: Augmentation Mammaplasty," brochure by the American Society of Plastic and Reconstructive Surgeons, brochure number 1255.

10. Personal interview with Tracy E. McCall, M.D., February 1, 2001.

11. "Breast Augmentation: Augmentation Mammaplasty," brochure by the American Society of Plastic and Reconstructive Surgeons, brochure number 1255.

12. "Liposuction: Suction-Assisted Lipectomy," brochure by the American Society of Plastic and Reconstructive Surgeons, brochure number 1254.

13. Personal interview with Tracy E. McCall, M.D., February 1, 2001.

14. Laurence Urdang, ed., *Mosby's Medical and Nursing Dictionary* (St. Louis: C.V. Mosby Company, 1983), p. 784.

15. Personal interview with Tracy E. McCall, M.D., February 1, 2001.

16. Telephone interview with Michelle Bonness, M.D., October 22, 2002.

Chapter 5. Making the Decision

1. Quoted in Karen Fanning, "Perfectly Plastic?" *Scholastic Choices*, March 2001, vol. 16, issue 6, p. 20.

2. Ibid.

3. Ibid.

4. Telephone interview with David Larson, M.D., December 14, 2001.

5. Personal interview with Laura Gray, R.N., M.S.N., December 21, 2001.

6. Adapted from Dr. Ann Kearney-Cooke, "Secrets to Self-Esteem" curriculum, quoted in Genevieve Belfiglio, "Teens and Plastic Surgery: Too Young to Seek Perfection?" n.d., <http://www.CBSHealthwatch.com> (September 13, 2001).

Glossary

airbrushing or computer enhancement—Techniques used to remove imperfections from people in photographs and make them look better. Airbrushing is done to the negative of a photograph. With digital photography, enhancement can be done on a computer.

American Society of Plastic Surgeons—One of the professional organizations for cosmetic and plastic surgeons.

anesthetic—A drug given to people having surgery so they will not feel pain. An anesthetic can be local, which numbs the area, or general, which puts the person to sleep.

body dysmorphic disorder (BDD)—A psychological problem in which a person becomes obsessed with a certain body part that he or she believes is ugly. Often the person believes that the body part is much worse than it actually is.

breast augmentation—A cosmetic procedure in which implants are put into breasts to make them bigger.

breast reduction—A cosmetic procedure in which breast tissue is removed to make the breast smaller. It is done on both males and females.

bruising—When blood collects under the skin, it makes a purple-colored bruise. Bruises after cosmetic surgery can take several weeks to go away.

cannula—A tube used in liposuction to suck out fat from within the body.

cartilage—The tough, rubbery tissue that makes up the outer ears, the tip and the divider in the nose, and other parts of the body.

chin implant—Something put into the chin to make a receding chin look larger. It can be a bit of bone removed from the nose or a small sack filled with saline solution.

computer imaging—Specialized computers can show patients what they will look like after cosmetic surgery. They are used by some plastic surgeons.

cosmetic surgeon—A doctor who specializes in changing a person's looks through surgery.

cosmetic surgery—Surgery done to make a body part look different. Sometimes the part is made smaller, sometimes bigger, and sometimes it is reshaped.

day-surgery clinic—A medical facility that is not a hospital, but where surgery is done on patients who go home that same day. It has complete operating rooms, but no patient rooms for people to stay overnight.

health insurance—The insurance that pays for medical treatment. Health insurance usually does not cover cosmetic surgery.

implant—A sac filled with saline (salt water) that is used to enlarge or reshape a body part. Implants are used in breasts, chins, buttocks, and muscles.

incision—The cut a surgeon makes in order to do a surgical procedure.

laser—A device that creates a beam of intense light. Lasers can be used to improve skin conditions.

liposuction—A cosmetic procedure in which a tube attached to a vacuum device is inserted in the fat layer under the skin. The fat is broken up and sucked out.

otoplasty—A cosmetic procedure to reduce the size of ears that are too big or stick out.

peer pressure—The pressure people put on each other to look and act a certain way.

plastic surgeon—Another name for a cosmetic surgeon.

reconstructive surgery—Surgery done to repair an injury from an accident or a birth defect. It is not considered cosmetic surgery.

rhinoplasty—A cosmetic procedure to reshape the nose. Commonly called a "nose job."

swelling—Body parts can fill with fluid, becoming swollen. Swelling after cosmetic surgery can take months to go away.

Further Reading

American Academy of Facial Plastic and Reconstructive Surgeons. *The Teen Face Book: A Question and Answer Guide to Skin Care, Cosmetics and Facial Plastic Surgery.* Washington, D.C.: Acropolis Books, 1989.

Brangien, Davis. *What's Real, What's Ideal: Overcoming a Negative Body Image.* New York: Rosen Publishing Group, 1998.

Gail, Susan. *Cosmetic Surgery: Before, Between, and After.* Berkeley, Calif.: Publishers Group, Inc., 2000.

Gaynor, Alan. *Everything You Ever Wanted to Know About Cosmetic Surgery but Couldn't Afford to Ask.* New York: Broadway Books, 1999.

Semel, George and Jeff St. John. *The Complete Idiot's Guide to Cosmetic Surgery.* New York: McMillian Publishing USA, 2001.

Tucker, Shaw. *Who Do You Think You Are?: A Handbook for Analyzing the True You.* New York: Penguin Putnam Books for Young Readers, 2001.

Internet Addresses

American Society of Plastic Surgeons
<http://www.plasticsurgery.org>

American Academy of Facial Plastic and Reconstructive Surgery
<http://www.aafprs.org>

Cosmetic Plastic Surgery in Teens
<http://www.plasticsurgery4u.com/teenage_plastic_surgery/>

For More Information

**American Academy of Facial Plastic
and Reconstructive Surgery**
310 S. Henry St.
Alexandria, VA 22314
(703) 299–9291

**American Society of Plastic Surgeons
Plastic Surgery Educational Foundation**
444 E. Algonquin Rd.
Arlington Heights, IL 60005
(888) 475–2784

Index